last dance

t. kilgore splake
25214 ash street
calumet, mi 49913
splake@chartermi.net

Transcendent Zero Press
Houston, Texas

Copyright © 2025 by t. kilgore splske.

Contents of this publication remain the intellectual property of t. kilgore splske. None of these works may be reproduced in any format, whether electronically or in print, without consent from the publisher Transcendent Zero Press or t. kilgore splske, except as portions in reviews.

ISBN-13: 978-1-946460-61-5

last dance

t. kilgore splake

Introduction
Dustin Pickering

splake's voice is the creative spirit declaring independence against our collective culture. His offerings, like those of Beatniks past, assert and declare. An idiosyncratic style is necessary for a poet writing in the murky environment of self-congratulation. splake's poetry stirs the waters to search for the protesting spirit within the human mind.

From alcoholism and suicidal desperation, splake is living proof that the poem is a lived thing and not merely "on the page." This is the meaning of authenticity. Poetry is a tool of protest and self-assertion against a world that ignores that "still small voice" within us that is also "great within us." In the words of Audre Lorde, "Nothing I accept about myself can be used against me to diminish me." Poetry is a creative measure that borrows from the the stuff of life and nature. Nowhere will you find this relationship as deep as in the poetry of t. kilgore splake. I am sure readers of this volume are familiar with splake's life story so it does not need repeating. The relationship of life to art is a volume in itself. Poetry also paradoxically creates and usurps life. In the words of Oscar Wilde, "Life imitates art far more than art imitates life." The creative prowess reveals and also creates the magic of life.

splake writes, "like driven poet's invisible creative muse" telling us that there is a muse behind this entire project of living. Something must stimulate and divine the world we in. In another poem splake reveals why he eschews titles, "difficult emotions with titles unnecessary". The frequent absence of titles suggests the depth of emotion splake induces and draws in his writing.

These aspects of his craft indicate that splake is authentic as a poet, human being, and person sculpting and shaping his life for himself.

####

poet lost in wild creative madness
words exploding from brain filling notebook
fresh blood covering blank pages

####

once pounding portable typewriter keys
poems mailed to editor with sase reply
book manuscripts submitted over transom

####

producing safe easy pieces of art
instead of taking serious creative risks
not feeling fear of failure

####

after early morning sex having quiet pillow talk
never talking about love like raymond carver couple
discussing new writing projects before breakfast

####

wannabe artist's voice slowly becoming silent
no more talking about stories and poems to write
shadow growing smaller soon no longer here

\# \# \# \#

twelve-step salvation
detoxing rehabbing souls learning
jesus easy to love god harder

####

artist moving beyond society's conventional values
abandoning religion motherhood flag and free enterprise
intoxicating feeling of being free

# # # #

death like bergman clock without hands
every day's time being the same
always empty endless nightmare

####

john muir and uncle walt
believing souls finding peace in nature
worshipping butterflies and wildflowers

####

youngster's worshipping comic book heroes
possessing mysterious super powers
like driven poet's invisible creative muse

\# \# \# \#

graybeard poems about past life
writing reflecting distant memories
this time getting things right

###

poet living quiet sheltered life
days writing like being lost on long trip
enjoying himself quietly at home

####

most people lost in dull empty lives
but after tasting creative magic making art
impossible being ordinary again

####

economic textbooks shelved in alphabetical order
reader graduating with master's of business degree
accountant wrestling numbers not writing poems

####

small press literary publications
important freedom for creative new ideas
producing books fascists want to burn

# # # #

many people born middle-aged
immediate accountants teachers clerks salesmen
never writing poem or painting canvas

####

black bare forest free branches
loudly rattling in dark november wind
coming into winter rorschachs

# # # #

serious artistic survivors
like singed moths floating
around creative candle flame

####

dogs continually fetching and returning
wagging tails and getting soft pet and treat
like most people always obeying others

####

enjoying life's fifteen minutes of fame
woman saying "i do" man signing for car loan
poet writing new words on blank pages

####

double-wide trailer park community
rotting pumpkins empty beer cans broken toys in yards
old harley and snow blower rusting in shadows

####

smoky paris bistro basement shadows
with baudelaire piaf and de beauvoir ghosts
discussing painful existential heartbreak

####

bright northern lights bouncing off clouds
illuminating lake superior and dark night sky
like stained glass beauty of god's heaven

####

poet's words touching lives and souls
writing about life death and passing seasons
difficult emotions with titles unnecessary

####

becoming hard of hearing with vision problems
difficulty walking and writing almost illegible
poet's energy fading losing creative power

####

sunday easter and christmas services
also with weddings baptisms and funerals
church members staring in phone screens

####

most people looking with eyes
lost in television cellphone computer screens
not realizing other ways to see

\# \# \# \#

pale birch trees
surrounded by spring trilliums
lost in sudden may snow

####

invisible route sixty-six highway miles
jack keroauc finally running out of road
lost in darkness of heaven or hell

#'

mediocre writer always struggling
dreamer quietly waiting for inspiration
his poem receiving a in junior high

\# \# \# \#

picking up wrinkled autumn leaf
noticing flawless design of veins
lost in god's wilderness creation

\# \# \# \#

escaping for wilderness moment
enjoying larger world of nature
more reality than computer screen

####

choosing present for lover
not expensive jewelry exotic perfume boutique certificate
instead writing romantic poem with words from my heart

####

autumn leaves blowing in wind
dancing dark rorschach shadows
like poet's life fading in twilight

\# \# \# \#

graybeard poet's quiet reflection
after devil may care exciting life full of adventures
wondering how much longer cheating death

####

mental health weekend holiday
tranny-tripping back roads smile on his face
hoping to get lost in wilderness

# # # #

son alone crying at day care center
growing up becoming semper fi lifer
marine corps becoming mother

####

macho man's big boy toys
4x4 truck powerful snowmobile harley big cc's
owning personal shit not more important than life

# # # #

graybeard poet's perfect life
days spent living in la-z-boy
with paperbacks dvd-player computer

####

late night early morning turning empty highway miles
turning off loud radio music for silence to think
checking rearview mirror to see if life catching up

####

following week of constant job stress
red-lining motorcycle over gravel backroads
hauling ass thrill calming nervous tension

####

college professor lost in academic shadows
desperately asking is this all life represents
like bellow's henderson's whispering "i want"

####

men crying not showing less masculine emotions
in tears watching "dead poet's society" movie
professor keating preparing boys for carpe diem lives

####

time before election and life after
memories of palmer's raids and joe mccarthy's ghost
waiting government detention camps for artists

splake

t. kilgore splake ("the cliffs dancer") currently lives in a tamarack location old mining row house in the ghost copper mining village of calumet in michigan's upper peninsula. splake has become a legend in the small press literary circles for his writing and photography.

splake's most recent publication is "yooper haiku" which is a collection of haiku poems written about michigan's upper peninsula natural wilderness.

presently splake is finishing three chapbook manuscripts – "soft core dreams," "beyond autumn light," and "pages whispering." he is also eagerly waiting for the publication of the new issue of CLUTCH, an avant garde literary journal produced by street corner press editor robert zoschke in sister bay, wisconsin.

for people interested in learning additional information about his writing and photography, they can connect with his computer site **tksplake.com.**

www.ingramcontent.com/pod-product-compliance
Lightning Source LLC
Chambersburg PA
CBHW061345040426
42444CB00011B/3104